T0065522

Looking for Love in All the Wrong Places Until …

Wilhelmina Carter

authorHOUSE

AuthorHouse™
1663 Liberty Drive
Bloomington, IN 47403
www.authorhouse.com
Phone: 833-262-8899

Published by AuthorHouse 02/09/2021

ISBN: 978-1-6655-1636-5 (sc)
ISBN: 978-1-6655-1635-8 (e)

Library of Congress Control Number: 2021902478

Print information available on the last page.

In Memory of my Grandmother, Martha M. Smith for all her knowledge and God given wisdom that she instilled in my life to help me to grow into the woman that I have become today.

Acknowledgments

I acknowledge and give thanks to:

Veronica Cooper, for her positive attitude about God's Word.

Josephine Parham, for encouraging the God-given ability in my life.

Brenda Lemmon and Yvonne Whipple, for being my faithful friends for over fifty years.

I would like to thank my cousin Helena Whittaker for her encouragment and artwork.

I also give thanks to Apostle Susan Lowery, who taught me how to understand the Bible and recognize the voice of God.

Chapter 1

Growing Up in Philadelphia

WHEN I WAS FIVE YEARS old, our family—my mother, grandmother, grandfather, sister, and I—moved from one neighborhood to a much nicer one. Families would look out for one another then. In the summertime, my grandmother spread a blanket on the front porch, and we slept outside. We could go to bed without locking our doors in those days—the 1950s.

Our mother moved to New York City to live with relatives. My mother was a young single parent, only seventeen. She and my father were separated when I was two and my sister was one. But our grandparents took very good care of my sister and me.

My sister and I had different interests in life. In spite of our differences, we loved each other. We loved our grandparents very much because they were always so sweet and kind. My mother and grandfather argued a lot. I didn't know why; maybe because she was such a spoiled little girl. My grandparents gave her what she wanted, not what she needed.

My grandmother always read the Bible first thing in the morning and last thing at night before she went to bed. Her favorite scriptures were Psalms 40 and 70. She read aloud, so we would know that God existed in her life. But we didn't go to church.

My grandfather had a very good job working for a company that built trains. Even though he made a decent salary, he and my grandmother ran illegal numbers rackets and sold liquor in the house. This was called a speakeasy, and it was a common lifestyle among blacks in the late fifties that helped them pay their rents and put food on the table for their families.

When I was eight, a fat white man would come to the house to see my grandfather and give him a lot of money. I didn't know what was really going on until I got older. The people in the neighborhood came to the house to play numbers, a form of gambling or betting on horses. If your horse won, that's the money you got for that number. The fat white man was coming to the house to give my grandfather a lot of money to pay the people who play and won on that number.

One time the police came to our house because of the illegal activity going on. My grandmother wrote the numbers on a small piece of paper, and when the police came uninvited, she put the pieces of paper in her mouth and ate them so that the police wouldn't catch her with the numbers.

Chapter 2

Devastated

I WAS ONLY TEN WHEN MY grandfather died in September of 1957. I was so angry at God. I asked, "God, why did you let my grandfather die?" My grandfather was the only person who loved me. He always made me feel so special. For years I blamed God for my grandfather's death. I loved my grandfather so much that I wanted to die with him.

We all missed my grandfather very much. He was a good husband, a good father, and a great grandfather. My mother and grandfather were always arguing. Nevertheless, they loved each other.

After my grandfather died, my mother started drinking more than usual. She was always cursing and yelling at my sister and me for no reason. She would beat on us girls for no reason. She would go to the kitchen, get a knife, and run us out of the house. I felt sad for my grandmother; she had to take the verbal abuse to protect us girls. When my mother calmed down, my grandmother would tell me and my sister to go back in the house.

One day I couldn't take the physical and mental abuse from my mother. I yelled out to my mother and called her a bitch. My grandmother was so upset with me. I could see the expression on her face. She said to me, "Don't you ever let me hear you speak to your mother like that again."

"Why do you allow my mother to treat you that way?" I asked.

My grandmother said to me, "That's my child."

I never asked that question again. My grandmother had an unconditional love for my mother, and even though my grandmother didn't get the respect that she deserved, she always taught my sister and me to respect our mother, no matter what she said or did. My grandmother was always a sweet and soft-spoken woman, and my mother was very spoiled. She was their only child, though she had a stepbrother who was killed in a train accident in New York City.

Chapter 3

Emotional Abuse

ONE AFTERNOON MY SISTER AND I had some friends over to our house. I don't exactly recall what my sister said to me, but it was embarrassing. I started crying and fell to my knees to ask God why my sister was so mean to me. Then my sister shouted in a loud voice to our friends, "I told you she was crazy." I thought when someone said that you were crazy, you were just different from anyone else (Psalm 39:13–14). I didn't care about being different; I just wanted to be loved.

At the age of thirteen, I found out where my biological father lived. My girlfriend and I were taking a walk, and I said to her, "Let's go visit my father."

"Do you know where he lives?" she asked.

I said that I did. I always wanted to know more about my father for myself and not just what others said about him. My sister could not have cared less about our father. If anyone asked my sister about her father, she would say that he died in the war. Out of sight out of mind. I always wanted a father figure (Psalm 27:10), but I couldn't tell my mother that I wanted a relationship with my father because she wouldn't have liked it.

My mother received child support checks from family court for ten dollars a week for me. He didn't send any money for my sister because he said she wasn't his daughter. I never believed that the woman my father was living with was legally married to my father though they had three children together. I wasn't sure whether they were married because my parents were never divorced, and that would have made him a bigamist.

During the fifteen minutes I spent with my father that day, the woman with whom he was living never came out the kitchen to introduce herself. Our visit was very short.

As we left my father's house to go back to my grandmother's house, I had a strong feeing of rejection. When we arrived at my grandmother's house, my father had called to tell her to keep me away from his house because it would cause tension between him and the woman he was living with. When my grandmother told me what my father said, I was so hurt. Was it my fault that my father didn't want anything to do with me? I never saw my father again.

By this time my sister and I were teenagers. Our mother decided to move back to Philadelphia with my grandmother and us girls. That's when things got worse. When my sister and I disobeyed our grandmother, she told us that she would tell our mother. And the last thing we wanted was for our mother to beat us. Our mother changed as a person when she was drinking. My sister and I had very long hair, and when she beat us, she would put us between her legs and crossed them so that we couldn't move. I always thought that I got more beatings than my sister.

At the age of fourteen, I was physically abused by two men. I thought it was love. I thought when a man told you that he loved you, he meant what he said. I didn't know they would tell you anything just to get what they wanted.

When my grandmother let me go out with my friends, I always came home late. And when I got home, she had an ironing board and a big belt waiting for me. She tore my behind up, but I still wouldn't listen. I wanted to do what I wanted to do. I was still in high school and wasn't old enough to go in bars. So I paid an older person to go into the liquor store to buy me a bottle of vodka. I saw my mother drinking, so I wanted to try it. After I drank the vodka, my friends had to take me home because I was so drunk. I couldn't go to school the next day. My grandmother said to me, "I didn't know that you got drunk." I said I didn't know it either.

It seems as though my mother would take out her frustration or guilt on my grandmother. I believe deep down inside my mother thought my grandmother took us girls away from her. Our grandparents provided a stable home life for my sister and me. My grandmother told my mother that we girls could come live with her anytime she wanted us to. But by then we were teenagers and were so attached to our grandmother we didn't want to live with our mother. We loved our grandmother in a different way than we loved our mother.

My sister went to a school for children with special needs. I attended a regular high school and really enjoyed it. My dream was to become a pediatric nurse or race car driver. I really loved newborn babies. My grandmother paid two of our older cousins to help me with my studies because she only had a fourth-grade education. She and my grandfather come from a little town in the south called Bartow, in Georgia. That's where most of my family was from, including my father. My sister and I were born in Philadelphia.

At the age of sixteen I dropped out of eleventh grade because I was pregnant. I could have continued, but I was too embrassed. Or should I say ashamed? I was always attracted to older men. I was looking for that father figure; I wasn't looking to get married. I just wanted a father for my unborn child. And I wanted to get away from my mother.

One time I was asked to have an abortion. Back in the sixties, women would have abortions at home or stick a coat hanger up into the vagina to get rid of the unborn fetus.

I was seventeen when I got married, and he was twenty-six. Many of my friends tried to talk me out of getting married, but I wouldn't listen. I thought I knew what I was doing. I thought this was my way out of my mother's abuse.

My husband and I lived with my grandmother until my daughter was born. My mother moved out.

My mother didn't like my husband. She knew that he was a mean person; I didn't see that. I knew nothing about marriage. Remember, I was only seventeen. I could only see that my husband gave me a lot of things, and like I said before, I wanted to get away from my mother. I couldn't see the things in my husband that she saw. I didn't realize that he was obsessive and jealous. I thought that I could still go out with my friends. One day I wanted to get out the house because I had just had the baby. I just wanted to take a walk. Someone told my husband that I was looking for my ex-boyfriend. Yes I was, but I didn't find him. When I got home, my husband started fighting and kicking me in my stomach. I still had stitches in my stomach from having the baby. What made it so bad was that he did it right in front of my grandmother.

After that episode I stayed at my grandmother's house for a while. My husband would say that he was sorry for putting his hands on me. We finally moved from my grandmother's house and got a small apartment. By then I was pregnant with my second child.

One evening my husband came home. He brought his nephew home with him. As we were sitting around talking, my huband throught that his nephew said something inappropriate to me. But he didn't. All of a sudden my husband jumped up and kicked me in the bottom of my stomach. I was eight months pregnant. I was so paranoid. When my son was born, I thought something would be wrong with him. I thought his head was going to be smashed.

My husband would always say that he was sorry, and I always went back to him. Not because of love. I wanted my children to grow up with a father, which I didn't have. Besides, I didn't have a job, and my grandmother wasn't able to take care of me and my kids. So I felt I had no other choice but to go back to him.

After I had my second child, I never wanted more children; they were a year apart. I still wanted to go out with my friends. My husband was so physical and mentally abusive, he never wanted me to go out with my friends. If any man spoke to me, he beat him up. In truth, I was too young to be a wife and mother. But when you are looking for love in all the wrong places, and not listening to your parents, you will find things in the world that you are not looking for.

When my daughter was eleven months old, she was crying. My husband went over to the crib and punched her in the face. I thought he had killed her. He told me later the reason he did that was because someone told him that he wasn't the father of my daughter. Both of my children are my husband's; that's a fact. My husband would hit first and ask questions later.

One day a friend came my house with her two children. She wanted me to go out with her, but we didn't have anyone to watch our kids. So my husband said that he would watch all the children that night. Neither of us had a car, so she called her husband to pick us up and drop us at a party. I told my girlfriend that we would have to meet her husband around the corner because I knew that my husband would get the wrong idea.

When we left the house, she didn't know much about cars. I knew how to recognize the car he was driving.

When the car drove up and started to get in the car, my grildfriend's husband asked me where my husband was. Before I could answer to say that he was watching the kids at our house, I heard a loud voice say, "Here I am." I hadn't realized that my husband had followed us. I just took off running. I left my girlfriend. I didn't hear from her for months.

My children and I went to stay with my grandmother. My husband kept calling for me to come back to him, saying he was sorry—like always. I went back to him again. Like I said, I didn't have a job, and my grandmother couldn't take care of us.

It had almost been a year, and I still hadn't heard from my girlfriend. I called one day, and her mother answered the phone. I asked if I could speak to her daughter. I could tell by the tone of her voice that she was angry with me. Then she said, "Your crazy husband punched my daughter in the eye." After that, our friendship was never the same.

About three or four years later, I received a call from my girlfriend inviting me to a dinner party she was having for her cousin. My husband was at work, so I asked my neighbor to watch my kids until my husband got home and to let him know where I was going. I was so glad just to be able to get out of the house. I started drinking, and when my husband came home from work, I would be intoxicated.

I took the bus to my girlfriend's house for her dinner party. I had only been there for maybe a few hours when her doorbell rang. It was my husband and his brother. When they came in, I introduced them to everybody. Then my husband looked at me and said, "Let's go!" I could tell by the look in his eyes that he was ready to start something. As we got to the front porch to leave, he turned around and punched me in my eye. That's the first time I had ever seen stars.

When my friend and her family came to the door, my husband and his brother were picking me up off the porch, carrying me to the car.

On the weekends my kids and I stayed at my grandmother's house. I never wanted to go home. My grandmother didn't want me to go home to my husband, but she would tell me, "I'm not able to take care of you and the kids." I didn't have a job, so I had to depend on him.

Chapter 4

Afraid to Leave

ONE EVENING WHILE SITTING ON my grandmother's porch, a young man from the neighborhood was walking and spoke to me and my grandmother. At that very moment, my husband was getting out of a truck coming from work. He walked up to the young man and started beating on him and tearing his clothes. Why did I keep going back? Because I was afraid to leave. I just wanted my children to have a father.

Another incident happen at my gandmother's house. I had I forgotten to get my daughter's coat from the cleaners because we were going to church that Sunday. If I had to go back home, the cleaners would have been closed.

There was a neighbor in my old neighborhood, and our families were very close. I asked him if he could take me to pick up my daughter's coat from the cleaners. I told him that I would give him some money for gas. On the way back to my grandmother's house, I asked him to drop me off at my cousin's house, who lived around the corner from my grandmother's house. As I was getting out the car to go to my cousin's house, lo and behold, who was coming down the street? My husband. He caught up with my neighbor's car and hung on the car, stabbing him in the face as he drove down the street. I was knocking on my cousin's door, and it seemed as though she was taking a long time to answer the door. When she finally answered, my husband came up behind me and stabbed me in my back. My cousin's husband was a cop and wouldn't let my husband come in.

I went back to my grandmother's again. After three days, I went back to my husband, again. And again, he said that he was sorry, and again I believed him.

He would come home drunk after staying out all weekend. He was an compulsive gambler. He had a fairly decent job at the public transportation company, but he said that he was always trying to get more for me and the kids. When he came home at night, I would pretend that I was asleep with the kids. Then I would hear him call me, "You bitch. I know you are not sleep." He would pull me out of the bed and make me sleep with him. I would be so intoxicated when he came home from work so that I could block him out.

One of my husband's friends and his girlfriend came to live with us. One time when my girlfriend came home from work, she stopped my husband from throwing me out of the second-floor window. I wanted to go back to school to get my GED, but my husband wouldn't watch the kids at night, so I had to put that part of my life on hold.

❧ *Chapter 5* ❧

Grandmother's House

WE ALL WERE AT MY grandmother's house—my husband, me, my sister, and her husband. She just had a new baby boy. His name was Little Lenny. My sister's husband was holding the baby in his arms. I walked over to kiss the the baby, and my husband thought that I was kissing my brother-in-law. All of a sudden, my husband punched me in my jaw.

I never wanted to go home with him because I always felt safe at my grandmother's house, but I did. He would always say that he was sorry. I knew if I didn't go home with him he wouldn't give me any money to take care of the kids.

One weekend my sister and I went to stay at my grandmother's house because she was going to visit her sister in Jersey City. My grandmother took my daughter and my sister's son with her, and my sister and I stayed at my grandmother's until she returned.

That Saturday night my husband's niece was getting married. I went with him to the wedding for a few hours. I saw that crazy look in my husband's eyes; he was like a crazy person when he drank alcohol. I knew it was time for me to leave. I went back to my grandmother's house.

My sister and I were watching television when the doorbell rang. It was my cousin and her boyfriend. They wanted me to go for a ride with them, but they wanted me to drive his car. I wondered why they wanted me to drive. After I started driving, they were in the backseat kissing and hugging. We drove around for a few hours.

When we got back, my husband was standing in front of my grandmother's house. My husband assumed that there had been another person sitting beside me, but there wasn't. My husband knew that I wasn't going home with him because my grandmother wanted my sister to stay at her house until she returned from Jersey City. He asked me if I could take him home. I said that this was John's car, so John, my cousin's boyfriend, said, "No problem. Get in."

My husband got in the car. As I was drove, I heard my cousin screaming, saying, "No, Sam. Don't do that." As I turned around, my cousin's boyfriend was slumped over with his head in his lap.

Before I could say anything, my husband said, "You shut up, bitch," and slapped me across my eye. I immediately jumped out of the car and left the car running. I ran into a torn-up building. I lay on the concrete floor, along with glass, cans, bottles, animal feces, garbage, and trash.

I heard him calling me. "If I catch you, bitch, I'm gonna kill you." I had never been so scared in my life. I put my hand over my mouth so that he wouldn't hear me breathe. It was so hot that night; it was in the summer. I still had on the white dress that I wore to the wedding earlier that day. I was sweating so much. At least that's what I thought. I wiped my forehead with my hand, but instead of sweat, I wiped away blood. I didn't know when he slapped me that he had a razor blade in his hand. I tore the bottom of my dress off and tied it around my head. I lay in that building from 1 a.m. Sunday until 7 a.m., until I was sure that he was gone.

I walked about ten blocks back to my grandmother's house. I was afraid to look in the mirror, so I took large bath towel and tied it around my head. When my grandmother came home that next morning she asked what had happened. I told her my husband did it to me.

She immediately took me to the hospital. I had to get stitches on my forehead and my left eye. The doctor said that if it had been any closer, I would have lost my eye. We got back from the hospital, I lay down for a few hours. I was afraid to look in the mirror. My face was all swollen, and I had a bandage on my face.

Later that evening, my cousin and her boyfriend came by the house to check on me because I left them in the car when I jumped out. I didn't know what had happened to them. They were coming from the hospital. They had been there all night because my husband had cut my cousin's boyfriend's throat with a razor the same time he slapped me with the razor blade he had between his fingers.

Chapter 6

Enough

AFTER THAT LAST EPISODE, I never went back to my husband. I didn't know a lot about God, but I knew he existed. I prayed, asking God to help me. I didn't even know how to ask God to forgive me for not listening to him and wanting to do things my way. I had to learn the hard way.

My two children and I went to live with my grandmother. I worked a lot of part-time or temporary jobs while living there. When my son was about three years old, my husband took him away from me. I didn't know where he took him. He said if I called the police I would never see my son again. He brought my son back after two weeks. Later I found out that my husband had taken my son to his brother's house. I didn't know where his brother lived because I wasn't that close to his family.

Then I finally got a better job working for the government. I saved enough money to buy a house. My husband wouldn't give me anything out of the house that we both shared. I had been buying furniture and putting it in storage until I could save up enough money to buy a house.

My husband still called me and asking me to come back to him. But my answer now was always no, not this time. My grandmother would take care of my kids while I went to work. But I was going out partying, drinking, and popping pills. When I was with my husband, living with him was like living in a concentration camp. I guess I was always afraid to leave because I was sure he would kill me. I was so afraid to leave I wanted to take my own life and also the lives of my children.

I finally had enough money to buy a house. My grandmother and I went to look for a house because I wanted her to live with me. She really didn't want to leave her house because my mother was still living there.

I lived with my grandmother for about five years before I found a house of my own. I was still working for the government, plus I had two part-time jobs. My husband was only giving me money through the court system, twenty dollars a week for each child. He said he would give me more if I went back to him.

I still needed more furniture. Since I didn't have a refrigerator, I had to use a ice chest with ice to keep the food cold. I only had one bed, so we all had to sleep in the same bed until I could afford to buy another one.

I had to get another job to help me with my bills. I took my husband to family court for child support, so I had to hire a lawyer. My husband told my lawyer if I went back to him that he would give me anything I wanted. My answer again was no. The judge ordered my husband to give me $40 a week for two children. He tried to tell the judge that he had three other children, but the judge wouldn't hear of it. My husband cursed and yelled at the judge. I think it wasn't just that he had to give me support money for my kids, it was more that he was upset because I wasn't coming back to him anymore.

In 1976 I paid for a divorce from my husband. By then I had slowed down from going out and partying, but I didn't stop. I dated a guy for about eighteen months. He wanted to marry me and adopt my children. He had never been married or have any children. I was so messed up mentally and emotionally. I thought all men were just like my ex-husband, so I couldn't marry him.

After about a year, I met another guy and let him move in with me. My grandmother was also living with me. He was a nice guy. While I was out drinking and partying, he took care of my grandmother. I really did appreciate him for helping me with my grandmother.

The one thing that got on my nerves was when he drank beer, he argued all the time. One night he came in arguing. I asked him to shut up, and when he didn't, I shot him in the leg. I didn't want to kill him; I just wanted him to shut up. After that happened, we stayed together for a little while.

After that incident I knew that I needed God to change my life, and I started going to church. As I sat in church, listening to the pastor preach, it seemed as though he was talking directly at me. What I didn't know was that the Holy Spirit was speaking through the pastor, letting me know that the life I was living was not the life God wanted for me. I couldn't wait to leave church so that I could get in my car and smoke some marijuana, even though I throught that the pastor was speaking directly to me. I didn't stop going to church, but I still wanted to do things that I shouldn't want to do.

When your heart doesn't live up to what God's plans are for you, nothing in your life will go right. I knew that God existed, but I didn't know how to have a personal relationship with him. So I started taking Bible classes to learn more about this God and more about why I was always looking for love in the wrong places. I started attending Deliverance Bible Institute. I worked during the day and went to Bible school at night.

After a while, I noticed that I didn't want to go out and party anymore. A friend came by and wanted me to go to a bar with her. I told her that I didn't want to go. She asked, "What's wrong with you?" But I didn't know. I just didn't want to go out anymore. All I knew was that I had accepted Jesus Christ as my Lord and Savior.

Josie, a friend at work, would watch me doing my homework at my desk on my break and during my lunchtime. She said that she saw my life change from a caterpillar to a butterfly. I really enjoyed Bible school. God opened up a new kind of life that I knew nothing about. I said to her one day, "Some of my friends seem to be so different. I'm not interested in the same things they are anymore."

Josie replied, "Your friends haven't changed. You have." At that very moment I realizes that God was changing my life.

One Sunday at church I noticed a church bulletin on the board. They offered counseling sessions with the mother of the church if you wanted to know more about your Christian walk. I made an appointment for the following week to meet with Mother Brett at the church. When I walked into her office and sat down, she asked me how long had been a member of the church. She asked about my children. I told that I had two children. Then she asked me if I was married. I told her I was divorced but had a man living with me. When she asked if I wanted to marry him, without hesitation I said no. Then she said very bluntly, "Get him out of your house." I didn't know a lot about obedience, but I knew that if I wanted to change my lifestyle, I had to sacrifice many things I used to do.

When I returned home, I explained it to Al, the man living with me. I told him I didn't feel right living together anymore. I didn't know much about the Holy Spirit working in my life, but within a month, he had moved out. He would call me, but I wouldn't let him come over. I had to try to be strong this time. The last I heard from Al he had gotten married.

I was celibate for over five years. Then I fell into sin again. When I met John, I thought that he was in a backsliding condition, but really he was worshipping another god. He took me to meet his parents and told them that we were going to be married. We even went shopping for wedding rings. Then about eight months later, he said that we should see other people. I said that I didn't want to see other people. I knew right then that there was something wrong. Whenever I called him, he was never home.

I finally caught up with him. I noticed a greeting card on his table, and it read, "Congratulations on your engagement." I asked him about it, and of course he denied it. I didn't have any further contact with him.

One night John went to his girlfriend's. As my ex-husband approached her house, her brother and my ex-huband had an altercation over his sister. Sam, my ex-husband, was trying to explain to her brother, but he wouldn't listen. Sam just happened to have a gun in his pocket, which he was returning to his brother. All of a sudden, Sam pulled out the gun and shot her brother in the head; he was prounced dead.

Sam was put on trial. His lawyer asked me if I could take the kids out of school and leave my job for a week to sit in court. His attorney said that it would look good to the jury that he was a family man. I didn't want to do it, but I did. He was sentenced to eleven months in prison. When he was released from prison, he asked me I would come back to him. Of course my answer was still no. Before the judge sentenced him, Sam gave his house keys to his brother as they shared the house.

Chapter 7

Thank God for Jesus

As I mentioned earlier, after I shot Al, I knew that I wanted God to change me. I didn't like the life I was living and I didn't like myself. That's when I started going to Deliverance Evangelistic Church. I stopped going to bars. It happened gradually, not overnight. I completely stopped drinking and smoking in 1982.

I started going to a Bible college in 2002. I received a BA degree in Christian ministry at Chesapeake Bible College in Baltimore Maryland. I also attended Gary Whetstone School, which consisted of thirty classes of bibilical studies. I received a certificate in bibilical counseling. I also attended Christian Stronghold Baptist Church in 1996.

One class that really got my attention was called "Blood Convenant." It was about unforgiveness, and God knew I needed that class more than any other. The instructor said, "If there is anyone here who is holding on to unforgiveness, here you will learn why. Forgiving a person is a choice. Either you choose to forgive or not to forgive."

It was like a light bulb had been turned on. When I left class that night and went home, I called my ex-husband and said, "I forgive you for everything that you did to me."

When he answered the phone, it was like he had been waiting for me to say those words for thirty years. Yes, thirty years. That's how long I had been holding unforgiveness in my heart. My ex-husband and I became friends after thirty years.

The Bible says if I don't forgive others, no matter what they have done, then God won't forgive me for what I have done to others (Matthew 6:14–15). My ex-husband went back to school to become a pastor. He had his own church for at least ten years before his health failed. He was in and out of nursing facilities. That's when my daughter decided to quit her job and stay home to take care of her father. My daughter took good care of him before his passing in September 2017.

I cried out to the Lord, "Lord God, what is wrong with me? Why do I continue to get hurt and disappointed?"

God spoke to my spirit and said, "My child, you're not waiting on me. You keep crossing my boundaries. You want to do what your flesh tells you to do."

At one time I was visiting many churches. I don't think that I was church hopping, but I was always looking for more of God. I just wasn't satisfied. I hadn't realized that God was always there for everything that I needed. Then I started seeing people, places, and things differently.

There was one particular church I was attending. The pastor of the church had assigned another pastor to oversee the church. I could see something in this overseer; he didn't have good intentions in overseeing this church. I could see something that just didn't sit right with my spirit. Soon after that, the pastor sent a letter to all the members that the overseer and his wife stole a quite a bit of money from the church, and they had gone back to Detroit, where they came from. I didn't understand why the Lord showed me that. I did not know then that God was calling me to be a prophet. At that time the only thing I knew about prophets was what I read in the Bible.

I was searching for more of God than what I had. A friend told me about a prophectic church. I had never even heard of a prophectic church. I went to visit the church, Gilead Praise and Worship Center, in 2009. As I write this, it is 2020, and I'm still there. My apostle Susan Lowery, activate your gift you are called to do. In the future she will have a prophectic school for the prophets.

I'm living a celibate and holy lifestyle. I like who I have become, a child of the Most High God.

As for my son, Tracee, by the time he became a teenager and on into his early twenties, he started hanging out with people he shouldn't be associating with. He wanted to change his environment, so he moved to Florida. At that time, my son was working for the circus in New Jersey, and he wanted to continue working for the circus in Florida.

Like his mother, after he experienced some life challenges, God eventually changed his life. For the last twenty-two years, Tracee has lived in Gainesville, Florida, and is doing well. He has a successful position at Home Depot and wants to be an entrepreneur. He wants to name his business after me. He also goes to the prison twice a week to minister to the inmates. Sometimes he has speaking engagements at other churches.

My daughter received a nursing certificate from Roxborough Nursing School. She continued her education at Lasall University, receiving her RN and a bachelor of science degree in nursing. She is also a biblicial counselor at her church.

My grandson received a bachelor's degree in nursing from Duquesne University in Pittsburgh, Pennsylvania, in 2013. He got married in August 2017 to a beautiful young lady he met in college. They don't have any children yet. They are both active in their church.

As for myself, I like who I have become and who I am becoming. I'm still growing in the things of God. I'm learning so much about myself and how much God loves me. The love I was looking for was always there from God. I was looking for love in all the wrong places until I began the righteousness of God. I've been redeemed, forgiven, and washed in the blood of Jesus. Who the Son sets free is free indeed.

I thank God for the good, the bad, and the indifferent; for all my trials and tribulations. I believe God will send me the special person who will love me for who I am, not who I used to be (Proverbs 18:22). Until then I will wait on the Lord (Psalm 27:14).

If God can restore what the devil has stolen from me, he can restore you (Joel 2:25). I have been rejected by my father. I don't have any bitternes or unforgiveness toward him. Even though I haven't seen my father for over forty years, I never stopped loving my biological father. That's how God loves us; he never stops.

In order to go forward in life, you have to ask God to give you the grace to forget about the things that are behind you and to let go of all past emotions, past hurts, bitterness, and most of all unforgiveness. Unforgiveness will hinder everything that God has for you. I know it almost took me off this earth. Unforgiveness will kill you.

I will continue to pursue the wisdom and knowledge of God with the help of the Holy Spirit. The more you read and study your Bible, the more you will grow and mature spiritually in the things of God. Then you can be a witness to someone else who is going through what you have already experienced (Timothy 2:15).

Through the years the relationship between my sister and I has grown closer. I would go visit her at home, and she would visit me. I would talk to her about how you could have a personel relationship with Jesus and how much he loved her. And that Jesus is the only way to assure that you will go to heaven and have eternal life. She was very receptive, and at that very moment, she accepted Christ into her heart. Not very long after, her health started to fail. She had to move in with her daughter, Michelle, who took very good care of her until the Lord took her home to be with him. Rest in peace, my dear sister.

Chapter 8

Young Ladies

A GOOD MAN'S STEPS ARE ORDERED by the Lord (Psalm 37:23). Let God order your steps in this life. Don't try to do it on your own. Take time to set goals and dreams for yourself. Continue your education; stay in school. Never stop learning (Psalm 37:5).

❧ Chapter 9 ❧

Single Women

Seek ye first the kingdom of God and all his righteousness shall be added to you.

—Matthew 6:33

Delight yourself in the LORD and he shall give you the desires of your heart ... Be not so anxious, nor impatience for anything

—Psalm 37:4

EVERYTHING IS IN GOD'S APPOINTED time. We are on God's timetable. Wait on the Lord to fulfill those desires of your heart.

Chapter 10

Teenagers

Always listen to and respect your parents. God gave you parents to guide you, to protect you. God also gave us parents to pray for us (Ephesians 6:1–3). Don't be in such a hurry to grow up so fast or want to leave home too soon because your parents won't let you do what they know is not good for you. That's because they love you (Proverbs 22:6).

Chapter 11

Divorce Woman

GOD HAS CREATED US IN his own image (Genesis 1:26). God says that your latter days will be greater than your former days, no matter what has happened in your past. Remember God is a restorer and a forgiving God.

God is a second chance and many more after that. God said in his Word that he will never leave you or forsake you, no matter what age you are. God is there 24/7.

Chapter 12

To All Women

ALWAYS PUT GOD FIRST IN your life so that you won't have to go down the road I had to travel because of my disobedience, bad choices, wrong decisions, and looking for love in all the wrong places. Don't allow yourself to cross God's boundaries. We all fall short of the glory of God (Romans 3:23). Don't ever think that you are too young or too old to serve God. Today is the day of salvation. Tomorrow is not promised.

It was a long hard road. If it had not been for the Lord, I would not have made it.

All are welcome to receive Jesus Christ as Lord and Savior. He will give you a new life, a life that will change you forever. Being born of God's spirit will make you spiritually alive (John 3:3).

In other words, you will belong to God (John 1:12–13).

Mom Ma

My grandmother was a very sweet, quiet, spirit-filled
woman who was affectionately known to many as
Mama. In the summer she would sit on the porch
with her close relatives. They would talk about the
good old days, when they lived in Bartow, Georgia,
in the Deep south. She had a deep love for her
family. She was known for her stewed chicken and
homemade biscuits. My grandmother would always
read her Bible the first thing in the morning and
the last thing at night, before she went to bed. Her
favorite scriptures were Psalm 40 and Psalm 70.

Ruthie   Marie

The beauty of their smiles is priceless
between my mother and baby sister.
I love you!

My daughter, Justine, was always a smart girl.
She always loved school. I couldn't keep her out
of school, even when she didn't feel well.
My daughter and I loved to go shopping together.
She always wanted me to teach her how to do
the Bop, a dance they did back in the 1950s.
She always loved children. She would take
most of the kids in the neighborhood to the
library and on on field trips to the museum.

My daughter Justine was always a smart girl. She always loved school.
I couldn't keep her out of school, even when she didn't
feel. My daughter and I loved to go shopping together.
She always wanted me to teach her how to do the
{BOP} it was a dance they did back in the 1950's.
She always loved children. the kids in the neighborhood to the library,
she also would take the children on field trips to the museum.

Wilhelmina

This book will help you to connect to the missing link,
so you don't go looking for love in all the wrong places.
I have always been a very ambitious person and
a hard worker. I love learning, especially from
older people. They have so much wisdom.
Whenever I put my mind to a task. I
won't stop until I complete it.
As a young child I wanted to be pediatric nurse
because I loved little babies, or a race car driver.
I like reading books that will help me to motivate
myself and achieve my potential in life.

Marie

Throughout the years, my sister and I had a beautiful relationship and grew very close. I would go visit her at her home, and she would visit me at mine. I would talk to her about how she could have a personal relationship with Jesus and how much Jesus loved her. I wanted my sister to know that Jesus is the only way to assure that she would go to heaven and have eternal life. She was very receptive. That very moment she accepted Christ into her heart. Not very long after, her health started to fail, and she had to move in with her daughter, Michelle, who took very good care of her until the Lord took her home to be with him.

I always been an ambitions person, and a hard worker.
I love learning, especially from older people.
They have so much wisdom.
Whenever I put my mind to a task, I won't stop until I
complete it. As a young child I wanted to be pediatric nurse
because, I loved little babies, or an race car driver.
I like reading books that will help me to motivate my potential in life.

Printed in the United States
By Bookmasters